WHOLE *IN* CHRIST
A BIBLICAL APPROACH TO SINGLENESS

DANVERS PRESS RESOURCES

Hospitality Matters: Reviving an Ancient Practice for Modern Mission

Building a Marriage Culture: Renewal in the Ruins

WHOLE *IN* CHRIST
A BIBLICAL APPROACH TO SINGLENESS

OWEN STRACHAN, SERIES EDITOR

Danvers Press

Cover Design by Morgan Taylor
Layout Design by Mathew B. Sims
www.MathewBryanSims.com

TABLE OF CONTENTS

1
RADICALLY SINGLE: AUTHENTIC CHRISTIANITY AS MEN AND WOMEN

Dr. David Platt

Over a hundred years ago, over 90% of the adult population in the United States of America was married. Most people married young. Divorce was uncommon. Even widows often remarried quickly. For the most part, being an adult was synonymous with being married. Singleness was rare. Today, almost half of the adult population in our country is married. Nearly half of adults have either never married, or are now widowed, separated, divorced. People are staying single longer than ever before in our country. And as a result of these things, single adults are almost as common as married adults today.

So what are we to think about this? Is this a good thing? A bad thing? What does Scripture speak to this?

Hopefully Scripture speaks better than we and the church have spoken. You look in Christian bookstores at books on marriage and parenting—and then compare that with books on singleness—their content is interesting. Very few marriage books argue that marriage is a good thing—that's accepted. Instead they talk about all the problems in marriage and how to deal with them. Christian marriage books tell you how to deal with the difficulty of marriage. On the other hand, books on singleness take a different approach. They almost imply that singleness is a problem. They tell a person how to make the most of the time until the right person comes along. In other words, they say that the solution to the problem of singleness is marriage. And then—good news —once you get marriage, you're going to have all other kinds of problems and read the marriage books. There's got to be a better answer than this, and Scripture gives it.

Paul, a single man, writes these words to a young church in pagan Corinth in the 1st Century. His aim, I don't believe, is to give us a complete theology of marriage and singleness. Instead, he's addressing specific issues and questions in his culture and in the 1st Century, but with timeless words that apply to all cultures and all centuries—including ours. So he writes:

"Now as a concession, not a command, I say this. I wish that all were as I myself am. But each has his own gift from God, one of one kind and one of another. To the unmarried and the widows I say that it is good for them to remain single as I am. But if they cannot exercise self-control, they should marry. For it is better to marry than to burn with passion." (1 Cor. 7:6)

Skip down to verse 17.

> "Only let each person lead the life that the Lord has assigned to him, and to which God has called him. This is my rule in all the churches. Was anyone at the time of his call already circumcised? Let him not seek to remove the marks of circumcision. Was anyone at the time of his call uncircumcised? Let him not seek circumcision. For neither circumcision counts for anything nor uncircumcision, but keeping the commandments of God. Each one should remain in the condition in which he was called. Were you a bondservant when called? Do not be concerned about it. (But if you can gain your freedom, avail yourself of the opportunity.) For he who was called in

the Lord as a bondservant is a freedman of the Lord. Likewise he who was free when called is a bondservant of Christ. You were bought with a price; do not become bondservants of men. So, brothers, in whatever condition each was called, there let him remain with God."

Skip down to verse 32.

"I want you to be free from anxieties. The unmarried man is anxious about the things of the Lord, how to please the Lord. But the married man is anxious about worldly things, how to please his wife, and his interests are divided. And the unmarried or betrothed woman is anxious about the things of the Lord, how to be holy in body and spirit. But the married woman is anxious about worldly things, how to please her husband. I say this for your own benefit, not to lay any restraint upon you, but to promote good order and to secure your undivided devotion to the Lord."

There are two realities that I want to bring to light from 1 Corinthians 7 for how we understand singleness in the church today.

1) WE AFFIRM SINGLENESS AS A GOOD GIFT FROM GOD THAT PORTRAYS THE GOSPEL OF GOD.

Paul says in verse 7 that singleness is a gift—and God doesn't give bad gifts. Singleness is a good gift from God that portrays the gospel of God. Now we're used to talking about how marriage portrays the Gospel, and rightly so. Marriage paints a picture to the world of Christ's sacrificial love for his church. The church responds in submissive and glad obedience to Christ.

The effect of this sometimes causes singles to think: "if I am to portray the gospel, I need to get married." While God does call many to be married, husbands and wives are not the only ones who get to portray the gospel to the world. The gospel, the good news that the holy and just gracious Creator of the universe has looked upon relentlessly rebellious, hopelessly sinful men and women and has sent his son—God in the flesh—to bear his wrath against sin on the cross, and to show his power over sin in the resurrection, so that anyone, anywhere, through faith in Christ may be reconciled to God forever. That's good news.

And singleness uniquely pictures this good news in many ways. I'll mention two. First, singleness portrays a Christian's ultimate identity in Christ.

The world would say "you need a husband or wife to complete you." But biblical singleness reminds us that this is not true. The Bible reminds us that we are complete regardless of marital status. In Christ we have been reconciled to God. Scripture testifies—Isaiah 54, John 3, Revelation 19—that the Lord is a husband to his people, more satisfying and more eternal than any other husband or wife could ever be.

In this way, there's a sense in which the supremacy of Christ and the satisfaction of God is uniquely and powerfully portrayed in singleness. Singleness says to the world: "Christ is my pleasure, and in him I have everything I need," in a way that marriage doesn't. That's why Amy Carmichael in her singleness once said: "There is joy, joy found in nowhere else when we can look up into Christ's face when he says to us 'am I not enough for thee mine own?' With a true 'yes Lord, thou art enough.'" Singleness portrays Christian's ultimate identity in Christ, and singleness portrays an eternal identification with the church.

We all know that familial relationships in this world—as wonderful as they are—are passing away. They're based on physical bloodline. But the church is based on another bloodline. And consequently, it's the relationships we have through Christ in the church that are eternal. Christ came to show us this, to give us a new definition of family. I've often wanted to preach Luke 12 on Christmas. "Do you think that I have come to give peace on earth? No, I tell you, but rather division. For from now on in one house there will be five divided, three against two and two against three. They will be divided, father against son and son against father, mother against daughter and daughter against mother, mother-in-law against her daughter-in-law and daughter-in-law against mother-in-law."

We know that marriage is temporary. Jesus tells us in Matthew 22, "In the resurrection they neither marry nor are given in marriage." Marriage is temporary but relationship with Christ and his church is timeless. So I want to remind married people: we're only married for a while—in this life. And for billions and trillions of years we will all be single. And singleness in this sense uniquely portrays our eternal state with Christ as a member of his church. So for these reasons, and for more, we affirm singleness as a good gift from God that portrays the Gospel of God.

2) WE EXHORT SINGLE BROTHERS AND SISTERS TO USE THIS GOOD GIFT FOR GOD'S GREAT GLORY IN THE WORLD.

The message of 1 Corinthians 7 to single brothers and sisters is clear: don't squander your singleness. Paul is definitely not advocating extending adolescence to ones 20's and 30's—wasting away at life on part time jobs and all the time video games. Paul says there's a divine purpose in singleness that must not be wasted in light of the times we're in. He writes in vs. 26: "I think that in view of the present distress it is good for a person to remain as he is." And he goes on to say in vs. 27, "are you free from a wife, do not seek a wife." We're not sure exactly what Paul means by "present distress" here. Most believe it basically revolves around two primary factors: persecution and perversion. Because persecution was rampant in the 1st Century it was not easy to be a Christian, and during days that add troubles, pressures, stresses that normally accompany marriage on top of that that would normally makes things harder. And then perversion was great. We know sexual immorality was rampant in Corinth. Paul says with urgency that the appointed time has grown short, and he exhorts single brothers and sisters in at least three significant ways:

First, be focused on the mission. Here Paul is echoing what Jesus said in Matthew 19, concerning eunuchs who have made themselves eunuchs for the sake of the Kingdom, which takes us back to Isaiah 56:3-5, where God says: "let not the eunuch say, 'Behold, I am a dry tree.' For thus says the LORD: 'To the eunuchs who keep my Sabbaths, who choose the things that please me and hold fast my covenant, I will give in my house and within my walls a monument and a name better than sons and daughters; I will give them an everlasting name that shall not be cut off.'"

Single men or women you are not a dry tree and your name will not be cut off because you have no children, for the expansion of God's Kingdom is not dependent on physical offspring, the Kingdom involves spiritual offspring. Your name will be better than if you had sons and daughters. This is Genesis 1:28 being ratcheted up by Matthew 28: "be fruitful and multiply"—the mandate given to the first married couple. "Go and make disciples, multiply children of God in all nations"—the mandate give to every single Christian to be focused on this mission. Singleness is for the sake of the kingdom.

Remember the world of Brena Taylor, single missionary to Kenya, who said "being single has meant that I am free to take risks that I might not take were I a mother of a family dependent on me. Being single has given me freedom to move about the world without having to pack up a household first. And this freedom has brought to me moments that I would not trade for anything else on this side of eternity." Similarly the words of Trevor Douglas who said "The first advantage of being is single is that it's best adapted to perilous situations and rugged life among primitive tribes and gorilla infested areas, or in disease and famine—the single man has only himself to worry about. Paul claims that being single and male best fits the shortness of the time. Doing God's work is a momentary thing. Advantages and opportunities come and go very quickly. The single lifestyle enables me to get the most out of the time God has given me for his work."

The Apostle Paul has scores of great men and women after him have been single for the advancement of God's kingdom. Their heritage is greater and better than even physical sons and daughters, for their heritage includes hosts of men and women bowing around the throne as children of God. Could it be, brothers and sisters, that in singleness, that your greatest impact for the kingdom of God will come not in spite of your singleness but precisely because of your singleness. Be focused on the mission, Paul says, and be undistracted in your affections. I want you to be free from your anxieties. Paul's intentions here is not to devalue marriage and all that married men have to do for their wives, or married wives have to do for their husbands. Instead he's saying to singles, unmarried men and women, you are free from this distraction on your affections. You're even less tied to the world than the married man or women—so take advantage of this. Now this is obviously not to say that there is no potential distractions for the affection of the single brother or sister. Be assured: our adversary is active. He is subtly working to undermine single brother or sisters' affections for God's regard. Guard yourselves against the constant sexual temptation in our culture. Do not reason with sexual immorality, thinking that God has designed you to engage at least in a little bit of sexual activity outside of marriage. Don't rationalize with sexual immorality, believing that in order to be fully human you must express yourself sexually in some way. Don't reason with it. Don't rationalize with it—run from it. Run from all sexual activity. All sexual desiring, looking, acting, touching, outside of marriage. The world is desperately in need of single followers of Christ who will counter the cultural lie that sexual expression is okay outside of marriage—even necessary for fulfillment as a single. Use your life to point people to Christ who never once gave in to sexual sin, yet lived the epitome of full human life.

So flee sexual immorality. And in the process, fuel spiritual affection. And, guard against the adversary's attempts to destruct your affections. Focus on the mission, be undistracted in your affection, and finally Paul says be undivided in your devotion. Verse 35: "I say this for your own benefit, not to lay any restraint upon you, but to promote good order and to secure your undivided devotion to the Lord."

John Stott said: "Single people experience the great joy of being able to devote themselves with concentration without distractions to the work of the Lord and there is much work to be done." Prayer, proclamation, this Gospel in cities, and our communities, North America, and among the nations. There are 6,000 people groups who have yet to hear the name of Jesus. Be undivided in your devotion to the church. Let us affirm singleness as a good gift from God that portrays the Gospel of God, and let's exhort our single brothers and sisters— alongside their married brothers and sisters —to use his good gifts in all of our lives for his great glory in the world. As we live, give, even lose our lives in anticipation of the day when a great multitude like the roar of many waters and the sound of mighty peals of thunder will cry out: "Hallelujah, for the Lord God almighty reigns." Let us rejoice and exult and give him the glory for the marriage of the lamb has come, and his bride has made herself known.

2
WORTH YOUR SINGLENESS

Grant Castleberry

Often times God will bring an amazing season into our lives when we least expect it. For me, it was the Spring of 2008.

I had previously spent four years in the Corps of Cadets (ROTC) at Texas A&M. During those four years, I lived and breathed the Corps of Cadets and all Aggie traditions—24/7! On top of that, I was involved in numerous campus organizations outside the Corps ("off the quad" as we called it.) I spent my last two years as an Aggie Yell Leader, traveling to every Aggie fish camp, A&M club, and Aggie sporting event you could possibly imagine. I gave the university my all. God put me in that position for His purposes, and I learned a lot, forged lasting friendships, and grew in my relationship with the Lord. My only regret is that during those two years, I didn't have much time to process—to think, sit, and meditate on the Word. There were so many events, places, people, friendships, late nights, "buddies," and NO PRIVACY—especially in the Corps dorms.

Before I knew it, graduation day had arrived. On May 12, 2007, I walked around Kyle Field one last time in my Senior Boots at Final Review (It's an Aggie thing), put on my Marine Corps Dress Blues and was commissioned as 2nd Lieutenant in the United States Marine Corps.

Shortly after graduation I reported to Quantico, VA for the Marine Officer Basics School. The next six months were a blur of Powerpoint classes, long "hikes" through the "Quantico highlands," field exercises, land navigation courses, live fire ranges, and endurance/obstacle courses. About half of our time was spent in the "field." The rest I spent in a small barracks room that I shared with five other 2nd Lieutenants. FIVE! Needless to say, during those first months out of college, I did not have much time to "think" either.

So it was a gracious act of God's providence to bring me to Pensacola, Florida for my first duty station. I was surprised to be going to Pensacola. There was literally only one Air Traffic Control spot designated to my company of over 250 lieutenants. Many of us wanted that one slot, but God in His providence had designated it for me.

The Marine Corps and the Navy Air Traffic Control training commands are located at the Naval Air Station in Pensacola. When I checked into the station in February of 2008, I was surprised to be given my very own Bachelor Officer Quarters room. It came complete with daily maid service, cable television, and a view of the beach! This was so different from the woods I had been trekking through for the past six months, and there was so much more privacy and free time than I had experienced at both Texas A&M and at The Basics School.

Each morning began at 5:30 AM with a run with all the Marines. We started our classes at 7:30 AM, and we would often finish for the day by 2 PM. This left me with a lot of free time. I did not know what to do with the extra time. I started training for triathlons and hanging out with people from my church, Providence Church. I also had time to think. I often spent my evenings running up and down Pensacola Beach, stopping to read Tim Keller's *The Reason for God* on the beach. But for the first time in five years, I was able to really think. I was able to process. I was able to meditate on the Word of God, particularly the Psalms.

And that's when I started to contemplate my singleness. Like many of you, I longed for a wife, but I didn't see how I possibly could get married anytime soon—I was slated to go to Japan for 2 years at the beginning of the summer. That thought worried me.

It worried me until one night in April. I was going back to Houston for a buddy's wedding. For some reason I could not get a flight out of Pensacola. So I drove all the way from Pensacola to New Orleans one Friday afternoon and then caught a plane that night from New Orleans to Houston. I had recently bought *Recovering Biblical Manhood and Womanhood* and had decided to bring it along. While on the flight, I read the first chapter, which was John Piper's chapter on singleness. I remember that while reading, I was cut to the core. I was moved by Piper's exhortation to maximize singleness. I was moved by the accounts of singleness—by people who necessarily didn't feel "called" to be single. As I watched the sunset over the Gulf of Mexico outside my window, a new thought dawned: I must leverage my singleness for the glory of Christ.

SINGLENESS IS A GIFT

One thing that I realized on that plane is that singleness is a gift that God gives to His saints so that they can leverage their time, energy, and effort towards serving Christ and advancing His kingdom. I realized that instead of feeling sorry for myself, I needed to direct my energy to His service.

That's what Paul said in 1 Corinthians 7:32-35, "I would like you to be free from concern. An unmarried man is concerned about the Lord's affairs—how he can please the Lord. But a married man is concerned about the affairs of this world—how he can please his wife—and his interests are divided. An unmarried woman or virgin is concerned about the Lord's affairs: Her aim is to be devoted to the Lord in both body and spirit. But a married woman is concerned about the affairs of this world—how she can please her husband. I am saying this for your own good, not to restrict you, but that you may live in a right way in undivided devotion to the Lord."

JESUS IS WORTH YOUR SINGLENESS

After all, Jesus is worth your singleness. A relationship with Him is more than enough to satisfy every longing of your heart. Though your heart may ache for earthly companionship, if you are a Christian, you already possess the most satisfying relationship in the universe. And this relationship will last for eternity (John 17:3). Every other relationship can be taken from you in a blink of an eye. Not this one. Jesus Christ satisfies. Everything, including marriage, is "rubbish" compared to knowing Jesus (Phil. 3:8)."

Jesus compares the kingdom of God to a treasure that a man finds hidden in a field. The man sells everything he had to buy the field and possess the treasure (Matt. 13). Jesus' point is that He and thus His kingdom are like that. He's worth our all, everything we have to give, including our singleness.

HOLINESS IS WORTH YOUR SINGLENESS

As I have often heard Dr. Mark Coppenger say, "God hasn't called you to be 'happy,' He's called you to be holy." Paul said that your holiness was God's design for your life before the foundation of the world: "even as he chose us in him before the foundation of the world, that we should be holy and blameless before him (Eph. 1:4)." Ultimately, God's design for you is to be conformed to the image of Christ (Rom. 8:29). Sometimes God uses suffering and difficult circumstances—including singleness—in our lives to further this process of sanctification. But remember that these "light and momentary troubles are achieving for us an eternal glory that far outweighs them all (2 Cor. 4:17)."

So please do not take your singleness for granted. Instead, when you feel lonely and when you long for companionship, remember that God is using the sometimes "lonesome" moments of your singleness to make you more like Christ. "For it is God who works in you, both to will and to work for his good pleasure (Phil. 2:13)."

A GODLY WOMAN IS WORTH YOUR SINGLENESS

If God calls you to marry, don't settle for anything less than a godly woman! I can promise you that a godly woman is worth your singleness.

And simply put, there are too many godly, single women out there who love Jesus Christ more than anything else in the world for you to settle for anything less. Don't settle for a nice, "Christian" girl. Wait for the girl that loves Jesus with all her heart, soul, mind, and strength.

How will you know the difference? A godly girl will be plugged in and serving in a local church. She will understand Paul's mandate that everyone in the "body" must contribute their spiritual gift for the edification of the rest of the "body" (1 Cor. 12). She will dress modestly, at all times (Prov. 31:30). She will be more concerned with growing in character than with being found "popular" or "alluring" by the guys. So look for the girl that is defined by "the unfading beauty of a gentle and quiet spirit, which is of great worth in God's sight (1 Pet. 3:4)." She might not be the prettiest girl that you have ever seen externally, and she probably won't be the one that attracts the most attention to herself on the social scene and on social media. But if you can find her, she is worth more than any treasure in the world (Prov. 31:10).

She will bless you more than you can imagine right now. She will be your helpmate and will follow you anywhere. She will help you become more like Christ, and she will be your most faithful friend on this earth outside of Christ. She will satisfy your sexual longings (Prov. 5). She'll partner with you in the cultural mandate (Gen. 1:28) and will help you fulfill the ministry God has given you.

TRUST GOD

God is sovereign (Eph. 1:11) and is working all things for your good (Rom.8:28). He will withhold no good thing from you...after all, every good thing is from Him (James 1) and He is the giver of all good things.

Please brothers, trust Him with your singleness and embrace this season in your life. Ultimately, Jesus is worth it!

3
STOP WAITING FOR YOUR FAIRYTALE TRUE LOVE TO MARRY

Katie Van Dyke

A lot has been said over time about finding your soul mate or the "one." Movies have been made about it. Songs have been sung about it. Stories have been written about it. Leading many to believe that there is one perfect person for you out there somewhere —someone who will complete you. Someone who will give you butterflies. Someone who will make you feel so happy. We are told from a young age that we should expect a fairytale love story. We are told that if we aren't with someone who makes our heart burst with fireworks we should just keep looking until we find the one who does. But what if this is not only unwise thinking, but almost completely contrary to what Scripture teaches us about relationships and marriage? What if we are setting ourselves up for disappointment believing in this perfect fairytale?

MARRIAGE IS MORE THAN BUTTERFLIES AND FLUTTERING HEARTS

We know from Scripture that marriage is to be a picture of the gospel. When Paul speaks about marriage in Ephesians 6, he calls it a great mystery that refers to Christ and the church. When two Christians come together in marriage, they are pointing to the relationship between Christ and his church. It is meant to be an unselfish, willing surrender of oneself in order to show the gospel and reveal God's glory. In fact, every passage on marriage in the New Testament is very clear that it is about sacrifice for another. Nowhere do we read that marriage is about completing us or making us happy. Ingrained in us is the idea that we are meant to end up with someone who makes our heart go pitter-patter, or all our dreams come true. But this comes from our culture, not from Scripture. For Christians, marriage should be grounded on so much more than sparks and fireworks.

Of course, happiness and strong feelings are a by-product, but not the main point. They won't sustain a marriage over the long haul. Marriage should be the means by which we are able to do hard, kingdom work for the sake of the gospel and for the display of God's glory. God sustains a marriage and uses it to display his glory to the world.

FIREWORKS AND PHYSICAL ATTRACTION

So what about fireworks and physical attraction? Aren't they important and necessary? In a lot of ways, yes they are. But I do not think they are primary, or even initially necessary, at least when it comes to relationships. I did not always feel this way, though. I used to place a great deal of importance on physical attraction and butterflies in my stomach. In the past, I wouldn't even give a guy a chance unless I was immediately attracted to him. I always felt it was a deal breaker if there was not a spark from the very beginning. Last year, however, the Lord convicted me in this. I realized I was waiting around for Thor to come pounding on my door with his hammer, and when a guy didn't measure up I didn't give him a second glance. I was placing way too much stock in physical attraction and not nearly enough on godly character.

Physical attraction and sparks are not constant or lasting. Sometimes they jumpstart a relationship, but over time these things can fizzle and fade, and often times do. No one looks the same over the course of their life, and emotions are fickle. When I look back on my relationships and interests of the past, I realize that all of them began with an initial spark or attraction, which ultimately didn't last. In fact, some instances where I felt the most drawn to guys, they weren't even believers. The Lord showed me the great danger of placing too much importance on attraction and sparks. They can be extremely misleading. There are more important and necessary factors that should be considered before I feel the fireworks. For example:

- What are his theological beliefs and biblical passions?
- Is he someone I could go do great gospel work with in furthering the kingdom?
- Do we get a long and enjoy being around each other?

All of these questions should come before we consider physical attraction and fireworks. Most godly, growing marriages I see now began with relationships where the physical attraction and sparks gradually grew over time because these other things were in place first. Lasting, Christ-centered marriages do not occur, nor are sustained, when physical attraction is the leading and primary force. Now, I'm not saying we should force a relationship with someone we are not in the least bit physically attracted to simply because they really love Jesus. But I am saying that we shouldn't discount a godly prospect simply because strong attraction and fireworks aren't immediately present.

A BRIEF WORD ABOUT SEX

I know there are many people who think marriage is all about the hot sex, even going so far as to say that engaging in sexual activity outside of marriage helps them know if the fireworks are there and will last. I think a careful reading of Scripture, though, shows us that this is hardly the case. First, if you are currently engaging in sexual activity outside of marriage, you are living in sin. You need to repent and turn from it. "But, Katie, we need to know if we are sexually compatible!" Just stop there. Scripture is perfectly and adamantly clear that sexual activity is to be between a husband and a wife only. There is no argument to be made outside of that. We don't have to see if we are sexually compatible with someone before marrying them. News flash: marriage is not about sex alone. Yes, sex is part of marriage and it is a gift. But it is not what marriage is all about. Like the relational aspect of marriage, the sexual aspect of marriage also develops and grows over time. Even sex is not the fairytale that Hollywood portrays it to be. It is vital for relationships to be grounded in something much greater than sexual attraction. It takes more than that for a marriage to flourish and grow. Don't base all of your hopes and dreams on sex and physical attraction. You are setting yourself up for utter disaster and disappointment.

GOSPEL WORK FOR ALL

Singles, we have such a unique and amazing opportunity right now to be wise with how we approach relationships and marriage. We should use this time to glean from godly marriages. We should seek to grow in our understanding of the gospel and the relationship between Christ and the church. Also, while we desire marriage and wait for it, we need to be careful not to waste this time we have for great gospel work. Marriage is not when we are able to really start showing God's glory to the world. We can do that now! Pray for the Lord to reveal ways in which you can do hard, kingdom work in your singleness. When he does, get up and do it! Let's not waste this time simply waiting around for marriage. Instead, let's use it for his glory and the furthering of his kingdom. And when a godly man or woman comes around, let us look first at the heart before we judge them only based on the outward appearance.

4

JENNIFER MARSHALL: CONTENTMENT IN UNEXPECTED SEASONS

RuthAnne Irvin

Jennifer Marshall is happy with the life she never planned. She never planned to be single in her later years, and she never planned a career.

During her senior year of college, Marshall taught abroad at Black Forest Academy in Germany, a K-12 Christian school designed for international Christian workers or business families who want a North American, Christian education abroad. While in Germany, Marshall sensed a more postmodern cultural climate in Europe and questioned who paid attention to changing cultural climate in the United States. When she returned to America, she pursued an internship in Washington, D.C. with the Family Research Council in Education Policy, and she now works at the Heritage Foundation as the Vice President for the Institute for Family, Community, and Opportunity. The Heritage Foundation, a privately funded organization, seeks to encourage human flourishing from constitutional first principles. Marshall said part of her job is to help articulate principles and make policy suggestions to Congress to help meet the needs of people in society, specifically the poor, and strengthen the current culture through promoting policies that support natural law.

In her mid-thirties, Marshall realized her life "had gone off my mental, expected map." Things were not as she expected. After college she hoped to get married and begin a family. Instead, she found herself single and working full-time. She began to see other single, working women in similar life situations. Marshall wanted to help these women navigate singleness and career in a godly way. So she began to research the phenomenon of extended singleness and the higher median age range for marriage in both men and women. As she researched, Marshall realized there was a lack of conversation about women and singleness, especially in the church.

"Christians need to wrestle with and apply faith to singleness in the church," she said.

This led to her book, Now and Not Yet: Making Sense of Single Life in the Twenty-First Century, written to help single women navigate singleness as a calling to be embraced for however long of a season the Lord determines. During this time, what was instilled in her as a child—work with excellence in whatever calling in life for this season—began to emerge in her writing. In Now and Not Yet, Marshall writes about life as a calling, not an orientation of marriage, singleness, student, parent, or other occupation. "Each season is a calling," she said, "and Christians are exhorted to faithfulness in each season of life." Marshall sees life as two callings: first, Christians are to glorify God in all they do. This thinking drives Marshall's career, church involvement, friendships, and other aspects of her life as a Christian woman. And secondary callings include vocations like teachers, accountants, writers, mothers, and other jobs.

"The goal of living faithfully in each calling is not to escape the tension of wanting marriage instead of singleness, but rather to live faithfully today," she said.

And in order to effectively do this, Christians need to mine the rich resource that Scripture provides for faithfulness in each season. This is what Marshall's goal is for Now and Not Yet, to give Christians tools to live authentic and content lives in a culture that promotes sexual promiscuity, selfish career goals, and other useless pursuits. "Christians need to encourage each other to glorify God whatever 'hat' they wear," she said, "learning to balance all callings in light of Scripture."

So as Marshall has continued to work and serve her church, she continues to grow in her understanding of faithfulness in each calling. Her church family at Immanuel Presbyterian Church helps keep her eyes on God, checking her desires and motives as she walks through life and work. Singleness for Marshall is not her identity, nor is her identity her career or church affiliation. She desires to live in each season with a conviction to serve other people and the United States well, no matter the task. Marshall also tries to hold her future plans more loosely, instead focusing on faithfulness in her season right now. This takes on a variety of shapes. Through her role with the Heritage Foundation, she serves poverty-stricken neighbors in need through policy reform. She also seeks to help the church relationally and physically serve the poor and work towards alleviating poverty together.

So even though Marshall's life is not as she planned, she is content where the Lord placed her. In all of her callings, she strives for faithfulness. She desires to hold life and her plans loosely, to glorify the Lord in her work through excellence and service. She wants to live faithfully in the now until the Lord moves her in a new direction, into a new calling, even if it is not what she planned.

5
JESUS IS BETTER THAN SEASON ENVY

Mathew B. Sims

SINGLE LIFE AIN'T ALL FUN AND GAMES

We sat across the table to eat and chat. We hadn't met together in a few months. My wife and his talked about designing their homes, what's new with the kids, and several other topics that interested them. He and I talked about the kids, our respective churches, what we're reading, and home repair projects. We enjoy fellowshipping with these friends. There's very few simple pleasures like meeting friends for good eats and conversation. I agree with Tolkien, "If more of us valued food and cheer and song above hoarded gold, it would be a merrier world."

For onlookers, the four of us sitting at the table might have looked like haggard travelers. You might have seen dark rings under some eyes, slouched posture, and weary countenances. You see being married and having kids is exhausting. I rarely finish a week where I don't feel spent.

I've heard several married folk say something like, "Oh I wish I could be single again, so I could do whatever I want." Or "Enjoy being single while you have no responsibility." Or "Wish I could watch football all day." Married men often idealize being single. Single people work, feel spent, and have responsibilities. I remember being single and there were many difficult times. It wasn't all fun and games.

MARRIAGE DOESN'T SOLVE ALL OUR PROBLEMS

On the other hand, a few months back I met for lunch with a friend who is single. We talked about work and his latest outdoor adventure. We also talked about our activity within the church. I encouraged him to use his gifting to serve the church and not just consume. He encouraged me to not be discouraged with my current busy season of life, but keep pursuing the good of the Church with my gifting. It was a great time of fellowship. He looked weary and rugged. This guy puts serious time into work and serves the Church and finds time to beat the wooded trails.

He didn't say it, but I've heard from several singles, "I wish I was married. Life wouldn't be so complicated." Or from a guy I used to disciple, "Once I get married I feel like sexual temptation won't be such a problem" (married men no laughing). Once or twice I've heard, "Once I'm married and have kids, I'll start spending time with kids and not be so selfish with my time" (in the context of serving the church's children). We've idealized marriage in some ways. Married people have complicated lives. We struggle with sexual sin. Marriage is arduous work.

DON'T FEED THE SEASON ENVY

It's so easy in one season of life to idealize another season or the season you wish you were in. The point is that both seasons—singleness and marriage—provide unique opportunities and challenges. One shouldn't be envied over the other. In some ways, the church may be at fault for this season envy. We often haven't provided robust answers to the questions singles have. Married couples haven't been transparent with our struggles. We also have not provided rich community where singles and married folk can gather together, fellowship, serve each other, and disciple each other.

And in some ways, our discipleship has been pointed at the head, filling up our brains with biblical knowledge, but we haven't aimed our discipleship at the heart of either group. We haven't taught singles that sexual sin is only defeated by understanding our identity in Christ and by loving him more than temporary fulfillment. For married couples, we've failed to understand exactly what the marriage covenant is. We've created marriage consumers instead of disciple-multipliers of gospel culture in our homes. A re-orientation of our discipleship would shift our focus from season envy to the person and work of Jesus Christ and the seat of our affections—our hearts.

Married men aren't envying single friends because their life is so much better or so much easier—but because we're not satisfied with Jesus. Single men aren't envying their married friends because marriage makes life easy—but because we're not satisfied with Jesus. If you feed season envy, you will carry that season envy into your next season of life regardless if it's marriage or singleness.

Jesus is better than marriage and singleness. We must understand that, and not just intellectually, but with our hearts. When that season of loneliness arrives in singleness or in marriage, we don't throw our hopes on another person. We are grounded in the goodness and love of the Father for us. We are free to pray and lament, yet firmly hold onto the covenant promises of God.

6
TIMELY ADVICE FOR YOUNG MEN (BY A YOUNG MAN)

Cody Glen Barnhart

Most people wouldn't call me a man.

I'm about to be nineteen, so the government sure seems to think I'm man enough to vote or join the military. I also pay taxes, and though I usually choose not to, I have to shave my face or else a poor excuse for a beard shows up on my neck. Still, though, most people wouldn't call me a man.

Lately, I've been asking myself: Am I that much different than other men? How many of the supposed "men" sitting in pews week in and week out could still be called a man when we hold their manhood against biblical standards?

Not many. Instead, we often take boys and put them in the shoes of leaders, fathers, and pastors, dressing them up as the men that they aren't. Most people, both inside and outside the church, make the assumption that by advancing in your career, getting a house of your own, or growing a beard (unlike mine) you have become a man.

While I can't speak from experience, I can speak based on the authority of Scripture. I can't tell you how it feels to work a nine-to-five or be a father of two, but I can tell you what God is revealing through His Word as He prepares me for all of those things in the ever-nearing future.

Here are four biblically rooted pieces of advice for young men that God has been showing me lately:

1. GO GET A JOB.

In Genesis 2:15, we see the first thing that God does with man. God takes him, puts him in the Garden of Eden, and then commands him "to work it and keep it." Men were made to work hard. It's important to note that this command was handed down to Adam before Eve was even brought into existence. God didn't create Adam and Eve and then say, "Hey chief, you've got to look out for her now!" No, man was working the Garden before he even had anyone to support him.

Go out and get a job. It doesn't have to be your career or a lifelong vocation, but you need to be learning how to manage money well and be a good steward of what God has given you.

2. GO PURSUE A WIFE.

Quit being complacent about finding somebody. Looking again to Genesis 2, God states what moms have been saying for years: "It is not good that the man should be alone" (v. 18). It's essential for a man to find a wife. Matt Chandler, in a recent sermon, discussed the dangers of a bored man—I think the same principles apply to a single man. The longer you wait to look for your wife, the longer you're subjecting yourself to, "sexual immorality, impurity, passion, evil desire, and covetousness, which is idolatry" (Col. 3:5). While these are certainly strong words from Paul, I think most young men would agree about how easy it is to let these sins slip into our lives. Singleness can be a means of service for God, but when we abuse it, it becomes a bigger hindrance than helper.

3. GO FIND A MENTOR.

I know some of these goals are out of your hands. You can't force a company to hire you, and you definitely can't make a girl want to date you, or let alone marry you. These are pretty major life steps, and it wouldn't be fair to expect them to happen instantly. That's why I think Scripture recommends getting a mentor, specifically some kind of faithful man older than you who will demonstrate what a biblical man looks like (Ps. 145:4; Titus 2). My mentor is a local pastor who has consistently been a part of my small group, answered any questions I have had about life or faith, and made time for me if I needed advice from someone who has been there. By having an older, more experienced man (by the biblical definition) invest into my life, I have grown in my walk with Christ. Mentorship is like spiritual fertilizer; the rich nutrients of your mentor's advice and experience better helps the Word soak into the soil of your life.

4. GO GET IN THE WORD.

A man of weak faith is not a man at all. How childish would it be to hold in your hands the very words of the Living God and approach them flippantly? To be a man is not to check off a list of do's or don't's; instead, being a man is about cultivating a life of fruitful laboring for God, physically, emotionally, and faithfully. Want to hear practical advice for men from Scripture? Read Proverbs. Want to learn how to love your (future) wife? Read Song of Solomon. Want to learn how to create a life marked by spiritual disciplines? Read through the Psalms and put yourself in the shoes of the speaker or psalmist. We have no spiritual equation for manhood, but we do have the Word, which is enough to guide us, train us, and sustain us in our journey together as men.

7

MARRIAGE IS NOT PROMISED TO YOU

Jasmine Holmes

Marriage is not promised to you.

This thought, meant to refocus my mind on the providence of God, often made me quake. Because I'm what's commonly known as a control freak. And the fact that the duration of my singleness was something so extremely and obviously outside of my control scared me to death. I wanted to be married. I desired it more than I was often willing to admit, and, though it was hard for me to confess, I feared that I would always desire something that would forever be out of my grasp.

I desired it for all the right reasons, I knew. I didn't have a fairy tale vision of what it meant to find true love. I knew marriage was work and that the lifelong calling of wifehood and motherhood wasn't going to be as easy as putting my feet up while Prince Charming recited breathless sonnets. From watching my parents, though, I knew that I wanted to dive into that beautiful relationship that emulates the one between Christ and His Bride, to reflect to a lost and dying world the light of servant leadership, joyful submission, and loving sacrifice.

And, yes, I wanted to know what it was like to be in love!

But there was something else I didn't want to admit: my fear, my need for control, was a trust issue. It was something that couldn't be erased by matrimony or any other desire I was clinging to. I wasn't afraid of being alone so much as I was afraid of the fact that I couldn't "fix" my status, that it was something the Lord had to take control of.

My fear was the symptom of a far deeper issue: I was sometimes so anxious to emulate the relationship of Christ and his Bride through marriage that I wasn't living in the reality of my status in that actual relationship with Christ. He was already leading me, and I was already called to submit to that leadership... even if it meant waiting for marriage. Even if it meant never getting married.

In my fear of never getting married, I would often forget the vastly more important marriage feast of the Lamb, and the broader calling of serving him. In my fear of never being a bride, I would often forget my vastly more important status as part of the Bride of Christ. In my fear of never falling in love, I would often forget the greater love that drove my Savior to the Cross.

I would forget how tenderly the Father cared for me, and how beautifully that care had been displayed through the death of his Son. And instead of seeing his providence in my singleness as a further act of love, I sometimes viewed it as punishment -as capriciousness. I traded the infinite, divine wisdom of my God for the finite, humanness of my desires.

That's what fear does, sometimes. That's what fear is: distrust of an all-wise God who always has my best interest at heart. And, on this journey towards the more important marriage feast, as I'm slowly learning to release my viselike grip on my own plans and my own timing, I'm consistently reminded that, when I fear, I'm trading the beauty of things eternal for the myth of transient fulfillment.

Marriage is not promised to you.

Not on earth, no.

But, through the sacrifice of Christ Jesus, the marriage feast that seals your status as the blood-bought daughter of the Lord of the universe cannot be thwarted. And that's what gives us the strength to deny present fear for trust that our Groom has our best interest at heart, whether earthly grooms follow or not.

8

THE SINGLE AND SEXUAL PURITY

Katie Van Dyke

It is no secret that sexual impurity is running rampant in our society. You can't turn on the radio or TV without being slapped in the face with it. This idea of sexual freedom is everywhere and, shamefully, even in the church. It's amazing to me how widespread it has become among young singles in the church, even those that seem to really seek godliness in other areas. And, even more shocking, is the fact that sexual impurity is in many cases right out in the open. In one instance, they are teaching Bible studies or speaking of God's glory. In the next instance, they are posting pictures and talking about their weekend get-away with their significant other. Single brothers and sisters in Christ, this ought not to be.

CHRIST AND HIS BRIDE

Sexual activity was created by God for marriage and marriage (of one man and one woman) only (Genesis 2:24, Matthew 19:5,6). Later in Scripture, Paul goes further and explains that marriage exemplifies Christ and his Bride, the Church (Ephesians 5:22-33). When you engage in any sexual activity outside of marriage, you are not just sinning against your own body (1 Corinthians 16:16-18). Even worse, you are in direct rebellion to the Lord and completely misrepresenting the relationship between Christ and his church. You are lying to the world about how Christ and his Church engage with one another. You are perverting and distorting this beautiful and holy covenant. This is a serious offense, singles. The gospel you claim to uphold and defend is actually being hindered by your sexual promiscuity. You cannot truly proclaim the gospel to this lost and dying world if you are engaging in sexual activity outside of marriage. Likewise, the ministry of the Lord cannot flourish in your life if you are engaging in blatant and unrepentant sin. Stop fooling yourselves. Stop making a fool of God. Stop misrepresenting and falsifying the gospel.

FLEE FROM TEMPTATION

Thankfully, our gracious Lord has promised to never give us more temptation than we can handle (1 Corinthians 10:13). He will always provide a way out. Of course, we are to be wise in our decision making. It's much harder to find the way out once we are in the heat of the moment. So, we must be wise and put up guards to keep ourselves from even getting into that situation to begin with. However, if you do find yourself there, FLEE (1 Corinthians 6:18, 2 Timothy 2:22). Get up. Get out. I don't care if you have to run down the street like a crazy person. There is too much at stake if you don't. There is too much damage to be done if purposeful action is not taken against sin.

FORGIVENESS

If you have engaged in sexual activity outside of marriage or are currently doing so, there is great news! Complete forgiveness can be found in our Lord. No matter what the sin, we can find forgiveness when we repent (1 John 1:9). It does not matter how deeply entangled you are in your sin. The Lord takes the repentant heart in its current condition and transforms it by his grace. It is not too late to seek forgiveness and to start living in purity before him. In fact, all of your sins (past, present, and future) are covered in the blood of Christ (Ephesians 1:7, Hebrews 9:13-14). Even further, he actually purchased us with his blood. Paul states in 1 Corinthians 6:19-20 that we really aren't our own. We have been bought with a price. We are now Christ's and our bodies belong to him. Therefore, I urge you to not wait another minute. If you have been overcome by sexual sin, seek forgiveness and turn from it quickly. Single brothers and sisters, let us flee from sin and chase after righteousness for the sake of the gospel, holy and pure.

9
SURRENDER, SUBMIT, SACRIFICE

Leanne Swift

Surrender. Submit. Sacrifice. I repeated these three words over and over and over. Not recently, but during a season of singleness that was particularly rich. I was one of those girls who struggled a lot with discontentment. But eventually something did begin to change in me. I was 28, which you understand, was pushing 30, and it felt like all my hopes and dreams were just not going to be a reality. I began to think that it was time for me to be okay with what God had for me, even if that meant I was going to remain single—and not just okay, but joyful. So I surrendered my desire for a husband. My heart of discontentment was replaced with a heart of submission to God's will for my life. In my heart, I even sacrificed the idea of being married altogether. I was living Philippians

4:4-7 in the midst of pain, for probably the first time in my life.

> *"Rejoice in the Lord always; again I will say, rejoice! Let your gentle spirit be known to all men. The Lord is near. Be anxious for nothing, but in everything by prayer and supplication with thanksgiving let your requests be made known to God. And the peace of God, which surpasses all comprehension, will guard your hearts and your minds in Christ Jesus."*

During that time in my life, the Lord graciously brought me to a place where I did rejoice. My spirit was gentle. The Lord was indeed near. I wasn't anxious. I was praying & supplicating all things to the Lord with thanksgiving. And the peace of God did surpass my comprehension, and it did guard my heart and my mind.

That was three years ago. It was a season I won't soon forget—a season that I hope every single girl struggling with discontentment will experience in her lifetime.

But what about now? God heard my cry, He answered my plea, I am a married woman. I am living something I've wanted for many years.

And guess what? I am again learning to surrender, submit, and sacrifice.

I once again feel the way I did before God slowly and surely brought me to a sweet season of contentment during the latter part of my single days. I have sunken in to a depression, my spirit has been anything but gentle, and the Lord hasn't felt all that near at times. I have struggled with anxiety in a way that I never have before. I've had almost no peace. My heart and my mind have been less than guarded; in fact they have felt more unstable than ever in my life.

Whoa, I didn't think that was supposed to happen after finally receiving the desire of my heart—the husband that God has prepared for me, a very dear husband who is learning to be godly (what more could I ask for?). Yes, he is dealing with his own set of struggles, just as I have been wading through the mire of mine, but God has been so good to us in and through all of it. And this is my response?

How did I get here?

I stopped surrendering, submitting, and sacrificing. Just completely stopped.

Even as I write, I'm tempted to excuse my sin in various ways. But that would do no good. I want to walk through this new season of life, truly repentant, and not holding anything back. I want to once again surrender, submit, and sacrifice—to my God first, and to my husband. I have come through our (almost two years already!) of marriage, with my head barely above the mire. At times I have felt so exhausted that I thought I would drown in it. My struggle was due to my wanting things my way, standing firm in my way, and not being willing to let go of my way. I have put heavy burdens on my husband to align himself to my way in my timing, or experience my wrath. My only hope for change is applying the gospel to my own heart, and learning to extend the grace to others that I so dearly treasure for myself, but rarely give.

Lesson learned.

Again.

Perhaps this has struck a chord with you, as a woman seeking to walk with God. We can all think of areas we can be surrendering, submitting, and sacrificing; something we're going to be called to do throughout our whole lives. I must have thought it sort of ended with the long-awaited fulfillment of marriage, but now I know (through learning the hard way) that it doesn't. This posture—these three S's—will bring much joy to our own hearts, to our husbands, and most important of all, to God who already delights in us because of his Son.

10
WHAT IF I DON'T WANT TO BE MARRIED?

Candice Watters

Question

I know that marriage is not for everybody, myself included. From many Christian articles I have read, it seems that young women are to live their lives in wait for their husbands to come. But what about we women who do not want to get married but would rather live in blessed singleness? Do we also have to live our lives as if we are waiting for someone who we know very well, never will come, or can we pursue careers and live our lives (while still obeying God's Word of course)? Just wondering because I know there are a lot of women like myself who know they are not going to get married, but would also like some direction and encouragement from time to time.

Answer

I think you're asking, "Is it OK to not desire marriage and not live as if I'm waiting on it?" It's a provocative question, and I'm glad you asked it. But you've also made several assertions and assumptions, some consistent with Scripture, others in conflict, and I want to address those first on my way to answering your question.

Hebrews 13:4 says, "Let marriage be held in honor among all, and let the marriage bed be undefiled, for God will judge the sexually immoral and adulterous." All believers, married and unmarried, are commanded to honor marriage because God created it and declared it good (Genesis 2:18-25) and because it points to a mystery greater than the covenant between bride and groom (Ephesians 5:32).

What we're not supposed to do is consider marriage the most important thing, without which life will be incomplete. There is only One with whom we are to be completely taken, and that is God. He made us, and we owe Him all our affections. To place anything above Him, to desire anything more than Him —even if it doesn't look like a metal statue—is idolatry.

Americans do love marriage, so much that they keep getting married, repeatedly, seemingly every time they get divorced. Andrew Cherlin's book, *Marriage Go Round*, shows how atypical American culture is in its near preoccupation with getting married. Staying married, well that's a different matter altogether.

You say, "I also know that marriage is not for everybody, myself included." You're right that marriage isn't for everyone, in fact, some are called to a life of celibate service. When the disciples asked Jesus if it was better not to marry, He said, "Not everyone can receive this saying, but only those to whom it is given. For there are eunuchs who have been so from birth, and there are eunuchs who have been made eunuchs by men, and there are eunuchs who have made themselves eunuchs for the sake of the kingdom of heaven. Let the one who is able to receive this receive it" (Matthew 19:11-12).

Jesus is clear that to remain unmarried requires a calling, or measure of grace, and also that such a station should be "for the sake of the kingdom." I would ask you, in view of this, how do you know that you won't get married? How do you know "very well, [a husband never] will come"? Why do you not want to get married? If you say that you are content being single and with the idea that you'll never have children, never have sex and never have the companionship and company of a husband, all the while feeling driven to serve the kingdom, unencumbered by the responsibilities of being a wife and mother, then I'd say you're following the will

71

of Christ who said, "Let the one who is able to receive this receive it."

If your reasons are other than that, however (whatever they are), I would challenge you to consider them in view of what Scripture teaches, as well as to pray to God, as Christ did, "Father, if you are willing ... Nevertheless, not my will, but yours, be done" (Luke22:42).

If the "blessed singleness" you describe is consistent with Paul's charge in 1 Corinthians 7:7-9—"I wish that all were as I myself am. But each has his own gift from God, one of one kind and one of another. To the unmarried and the widows I say that it is good for them to remain single as I am"— then, yes, it is wonderful to live contentedly in that state with no eye to a future wedding. But if you're tired of all the "marriage is good" messages you read online and hear in church and frustrated that it seems to be happening for everyone but you and your friends, then I'd urge you to reconsider your rationale.

Marriage is, by design, for God's glory and our good.

When asked, "Which commandment is the most important of all?" Jesus answered, "The most important is, 'Hear, O Israel: The Lord our God, the Lord is one. And you shall love the Lord your God with all your heart and with all your soul and with all your mind and with all your strength.' The second is this:

'You shall love your neighbor as yourself.' There is no other commandment greater than these" (Mark 12:28-31). Whether married or single, we're called to live as unto the Lord, to work as unto Him, in community with fellow believers, serving one another, loving one another and laying our lives down for one another. It's not enough to "still obey God's Word of course" while pursuing your career and living your life, if by that you mean to make your desires your focus. But that's true for married believers, too. Whatever we're called to, whether marriage or celibate service, we must make God's glory our goal. Last night I was reading N.D. Wilson's *Notes from the Tilt-a-Whirl*, and this summation of Augustine's philosophy jumped off the page:

St. Augustine: Love God and do as you please. If you love Him, then you love holiness. What you please shouldn't present a problem.

The Christian life is a daily, all-consuming (Mark 12:30), life-directing (Colossians 3:23), sacrificial one that is others-directed (Mark 9:35, Philippians 2:3)—regardless of your marital status. Whether a Mrs. or a Miss, you are called to live for God, acknowledging Him as Maker and giving Him the praise He's due.

By Grace Alone,
CANDICE WATTERS

11
SANCTIFICATION IS FOR SINGLE PEOPLE TOO

Jessalyn Hutto

Hang around enough married gals with kids and you are bound to hear (on more than one occasion), "Oh, nothing will sanctify you like children will!" or "I didn't know how sinful I was until I got married!" After hearing this over and over again, one might come to the conclusion that God has indeed made some higher plan of edification available to those who have received the blessing of a husband or children. One might be tempted to conclude that until you find yourself in such a situation you are destined to remain in your selfish, self-absorbed ways. One might even assume that until the Lord chooses to use these super tools on you, your sisters in the faith will consistently walk ahead of you on the road to sanctification.

Are they being conformed into the image of Christ faster than you? Do they experience greater fellowship with the Lord because of their station in life? Have they not only been blessed with a husband and children, but with a higher level of spirituality?

Of course the answer to all of these questions is a resounding "no." Yet when the married women and mothers in your life share the incredible ways the Lord is using their circumstances to shape their walk with the Lord, they may unintentionally leave you wondering if he can do the same for you even without a husband or children. It can be easy to forget that God promises to us all things for the good of those who love him (Rom. 8:28). And for what good does he use all things (including singleness, marriage, children, and family) in your life? He wants us to receive the ultimate good through this—being conformed into the image of his son, Jesus (Rom. 8:29).

GOD HAS A VARIETY OF TOOLS

Every act of God's providence is meant to refine his children. Certainly married women are continually being sanctified by their relationships with their husbands. Of course mothers have to rely heavily, every day on their Savior in order to care for the little ones he has entrusted to them. These are real and powerful tools in our heavenly Father's hands as he seeks to conform women to the image of Christ, but they are not his only tools. He uses all things.

He uses jobs, classes, mid-term papers, family, boyfriends, fiancés, roommates, the church body, illnesses, persecution, longings and so much more to bring about change in his daughters. Above all he uses his holy word to pierce our hearts and teach us his ways.

GOD'S WORK IN ALL OF OUR LIVES

If our God is infinitely wise and perfectly good, then we must embrace the circumstances we find ourselves in and trust that he will use them for his glory and our sanctification. He is intimately involved in each of our lives and in everything works to conform us to the image of his Son. He isn't just working in the lives of wives and mothers, he is working in your life as well. Just as he uses husbands and children to sanctify them, he uses other means to sanctify you. You are not a second class Christian, the fruit of the gospel does not rely on your getting married or having children.

The perfect life that Jesus lived, the atoning death that he died, and his powerful resurrection from the dead, are all the basis for our sanctification. These truths are all that is necessary for us to draw near to our God every single day. This gospel is the foundation for our growth in holiness and what each of us–married, mothers, and singles–must learn to live in if we ever hope to put off the old self and to put on Christ. He may use different means to impart his sanctifying grace to each of us, but it all flows from the same life-giving work of or Savior.

So the next time you hear someone say, "Nothing will sanctify you like…" and you are tempted to think the Father has forgotten about you, speak truth into your own heart. Remind yourself that there is nothing that sanctifies like the blood of Christ. And that is all you need. He will be faithful to present you pure and blameless through the perfectly wise and good means he has appointed for you (Col. 1:21-22).

12

LOVE FOR GOD AND A DESIRE FOR MARRIAGE: ARE THEY AT ODDS?

Brittany Lind

Everyday I saw it. Pinned to my purple, polka dotted bulletin board in my freshmen dorm room was the quote:

> *Everyone longs to give themselves completely to someone. To have a deep soul relationship with another, to be loved thoroughly and exclusively. But God to the Christian says, "No, not until you're satisfied and fulfilled and content with living loved by Me alone and giving yourself totally and unreservedly to Me.*

*Not until you have an intensely personal
and unique relationship with Me alone.*

Something about this quote resonated deeply with my heart. I was nineteen years old and I knew I wanted to be married one day. I longed for that "deep soul relationship with another" but I also wanted to love God with all of my heart. I wanted to be completely satisfied in his love for me in Christ. But according to this quote, these two things were at odds. I had to choose.

Either I want a husband or I want God, so I thought. Therefore, I became determined to rid myself of any marriage wishes. I tried to give myself "totally and unreservedly" to God, like the quote prescribes. After all, it's only when I do this that God would give me a husband. It became a daunting formula: achieve contentment in the Lord while I am single and God will reward me with marriage.

A HOPELESS PURSUIT

There were times when it felt like I was getting the hang of it. I could muster up enough will-power to make it days and weeks —sometimes a whole month—without thinking about my dreams to be a wife and mother. Petrified that it would become an idol in my heart, I kept myself from admitting to anyone my hopes of being married. If Jesus was my everything, of course I didn't need marriage. But inevitably I began to crumble into despair. My desire to marry only persisted, and the more it persisted, the more it felt as though I was losing ground in my relationship with God.

It was a hopeless pursuit, one that I was sure to lose—until I began to realize that this way of seeing marriage was flawed. What if my desire to be married was from God? What if marriage was his design? What if it was a blessing aimed at making me more like Jesus?

In her book *Get Married: What Women Can Do to Help it Happen*, Candice Watters offers aid to women wrestling with this very thing. She wrote: "The 'marriage as idol' warning prevents many young women from gratefully sharing in what God created as good. And the harder it is to marry well, the more likely it is women will accept the cultural counterfeits-premarital sex, endless youth, self-centered singleness-falling into true idolatry of the heart." She goes on to explain that if marriage is viewed biblically, the sacrifice and commitment required puts God and His ways above all and it is unlikely that a godly woman's desire for a biblical marriage would become an idol.

In no way is this condoning idolatry or worshipping marriage as god; but often women spend much of their time and emotional energy beating down their desire for marriage, afraid that it may become an idol. Instead, if the desire to marry was embraced and submitted to the Lord in trust, that energy could be channeled towards growing in an understanding of what a God-glorifying marriage looks like and asking in faith that the Lord would provide the good gift in His wise and perfect timing.

GOD'S GOOD DESIGN

God designed marriage before the fall. In the opening chapter of her book, Candice draws attention to this and discusses how before sin entered the world, Adam would have been in the perfect position for fulfillment in God alone. Before God created Eve, it was just Adam with the triune God in an unbroken world. To go by the logic of my dorm room quote, everything would have been set in place for him to give himself "totally and unreservedly" to God. But that is not how the story goes. Man solo, reflecting the image of God as he does, still doesn't reflect the gospel picture like man and woman do together. In Genesis 2:18, for the first time God declared that something was not good-for man to be alone.

The problem is solved in verse 22 when God creates Eve and brings her to the man in the first "wedding" of the Bible. God created man and woman to be together as husband

and wife. We are not creatures of isolation, but of community. Even for those who have been given the gift of singleness and do not burn with passion like Paul describes in 1 Corinthians 7:9, it is not good for them to be alone. The communal God of Father, Son, and Spirit created us as relational beings that need one another, we are a body with many parts (1 Corinthians 12:12-31). Together, as a body, we more fully display the Triune God who made us and it is uniquely within the union of marriage that God's image-bearers display the glorious picture of Christ and the church.

Is it okay to desire marriage?

I repeat, it is okay to desire marriage. It does not mean that you are less godly than those who seemingly do not and it also does not mean that you need to obtain a certain level of holiness before that desire is allowed or granted. Marriage is always a gift. God doesn't do works-righteousness, not in salvation and not in matrimony.

If you are not yet married but desire to be, place your desire in the hands of the Father who, because of Jesus, delights to give good gifts to his children. Marriage can become an idol, so as Watters suggests, ask God to give you a vision for the sacrifice and commitment required and run to God who gives grace and forgiveness. Even still, although it feels risky, ask him for that gift. When your heart aches

83

from not yet having received the good gift that you desire, go to him and take hold of his promises. Marriage is a good desire and God is a good God who is worthy of our trust.

13
THE GOD WHO KNOWS THE END OF YOUR SINGLENESS[1]

Carolyn McCulley

The 12-year-old boy strode across the conference stage with complete assurance, oozing the precocious seriousness of youth that can strike adults as charmingly amusing. But any patronizing thoughts present were soon squashed, as 3,000 adults heard the evangelistic heartbeat of God in the words of the young speaker. After giving his testimony of being adopted from a Romanian orphanage by his American parents and his subsequent adoption into the family of God when he trusted Jesus for his salvation, Gabriel Spiro outlined his hopes for his future.

---

[1] Reprinted from the magazine *Joyful Woman*

Since becoming a Christian, I've had the dream to attend the PDI Pastors College," he said to spontaneous, thunderous applause. "I feel like God has called me to be trained and equipped so that I can go and help the poor people and the orphans that are still living in Romania. My desire is to start a PDI church there in Romania. I thank God that He has brought me to my family and to Covenant Life Church—my extended family. I pray that by His grace I'll be able to be trained in character in order to fulfill the calling of God.

Watching from the back row that steamy May evening, I gave silent thanks to God for the plans He has for singles and families alike. Eight years earlier, a single woman from my church had wrestled with God as He called her to overlook her own desires for marriage and children in order to serve a good friend during an international adoption process by traveling with her to Romania. "What would I gain?!" Charlotte Ennis recalls. "I'd have to spend my own money, put myself at personal risk, and watch someone else return with children. I would return with ... nothing."

Then 36, Charlotte was not certain that God did have marriage and a family in her future. It certainly had been a long wait and her hope was waning. She had no idea that she was facilitating the adoption of a child whose presence would be a blessing to many more than his own family. She had no idea that this little boy would develop a strong passion for the local church before he even hit his teens, and that he would be a regular and fruitful part of his church's evangelism ministry. She had no idea that one day this little boy would speak to a gathering of churches about their collective mission—and be the highlight of the evening. Nor did Charlotte know that on the same evening Gabriel spoke, she would be married—a gift from God to her at age 39—and the mother of several children.

But the One who "makes known the end from the beginning" (Isaiah 46:10) knew all of this, and it was His perfect plan that had been operating all along.

Moments like these are glimpses of the Lord's sovereignty in action—and treasures to be stored up in the hearts of single women, especially. Only occasionally do we have the privilege of seeing so clearly how "in all things God works for the good of those who love him, who have been called according to His purpose" (Romans 8:28). We should cherish and retell those evidences of God's grace to encourage and strengthen each other. Our Lord is not a random God: His plan includes blessing us, but also making us a blessing to others.

I didn't know Charlotte when she was single, but I do remember reading her testimony in our ministry magazine, one that was written just weeks prior to her wedding. At the time, I was 32, a fairly new Christian, and—to be unflatteringly honest -- horrified at the prospect of having to wait until 39 to be married. Now I am 37, a little less arrogant (hopefully), and grateful for Charlotte's example. Last year in my church, a woman got married for the first time at 43. That pushed Charlotte's benchmark out of the way and gave me six more years to hope, so to speak!

In my extended season of singleness, I've had the time to ponder the risks and rewards of singleness from the perspective of both a rank unbeliever in my twenties and as a chaste Christian in my thirties. As I write this, I have been praying over the demise of two Christian marriages I thought were trophies of God's grace—both of which were shipwrecked over sexual sin committed by the husbands. Many years ago, one of the men had asked me out. I had declined the relationship, and he went on to marry someone else while I remained single. But now I grieve for his wife and daughters as they wrestle with the nuclear fallout of a perverse and unlawful form of sexual sin. Though I do not mean to imply that God wasn't good for allowing this woman to marry my friend, I can certainly see where He spared me the "many troubles in this life" (1 Corinthians 7:28b) in marriage by keeping me single and unencumbered. Three times so far I've been privileged to see why He said no to my prayers asking Him for specific men to be my husband. In each case, it wasn't too many years later that I discovered I had been spared inheriting some serious sexual sin. That is one of the benefits of being an older single—I've lived long enough to see what unconfessed and unrepentant sin does to wreck the dream of living "happily ever after." Those sad moments make me appreciate the pleasant places where my boundary lines have fallen (Psalm 16:6).

Why is knowing God and embracing His sovereignty so important when we're single? We have to keep in mind that we've received this gift of singleness from the pierced hand of the One who bore all of our sins—from unbelief as singles to selfishness as marrieds. We can be like Peter who initially rebuked Jesus for His humiliating, yet glorious, plan of redemption—or we can be like Mary, who came to accept His plan and purposes, and demonstrated it in the costly outpouring of perfume in anticipation of his burial.

Confident of the Lord's good plan for our lives, we can emulate Mary and spend our treasures (youth, dreams, desires) to further His purposes on this earth.

More importantly, when we are almost faint under the strain and worry of wondering if singleness is to be forever, we need to be reminded that there is an end to singleness: One day we will be at the wedding feast of the Lamb and we will be His bride. Even if we receive the gift of marriage on this side of heaven, that's not our ultimate goal. It is a shadow and a type of what is planned for eternity and, like all things on this earth, it will have its conclusion in death. Our Father knows the time when earthly gifts will be distributed and when they will be no more; He knows, as well, when the heavenly wedding feast will commence. We can blissfully rest in the knowledge that the future is better than anything we think we've missed now: Jesus is preparing us for the eternal rewards and eternal joys of a future He's told us is too inexpressible for us to understand. For His purposes, and within His covenant to always do us good (Jeremiah 33:40), He has declared for us that being single now and into the foreseeable future is His very best. He desires that we overflow with hope as we trust in him (Romans 15:13) and his sovereignty in this season -- redefining hope from hoping in a particular gift from God to trusting the God of hope unreservedly.

14
5 REASONS WHY PURSUING MARRIAGE IS STILL A GOOD THING

Greg Gibson

Not to beat the proverbial dead horse, but getting married is still a good thing.

So, now that I have my conclusion out of the way, let me tell you why getting married at a young age is such a formidable joy. Let me note first, though, that marriage is not necessarily a mark of *having arrived.* I know many men and women who practice manhood and womanhood at a high degree in their singleness.

Nonetheless, I digress...

ONE: IT PROVES OUR PURSUIT OF MATURE MANHOOD AND WOMANHOOD.

Much like how our works prove our faith (Jas. 2:17-18), the pursuit of adult things prove our desire to mature as men and women (1 Cor. 13:11). The opposite of being a child—or adolescent in our culture—is maturity. As men, we are called to pursue mature manhood, and likewise women in their pursuit of womanhood.

Mature manhood and womanhood are marked by the pursuit of mature things. That might seem redundant, but it can't be stated enough. The gospel beckons us all to intentional pursuits. After all, it is the fullness of Christ we are chasing after in our sanctification (Eph. 4:13). And marriage is a great discipline in our sanctification.

If we want to pursue maturity, then we have to practice consistency. And as a young person, the pursuit of marriage is a great mark of your pursuit of mature manhood and womanhood.

TWO: IT PROVES OUR DEPENDENCY ON GOD.

When my wife and I married, I had $15.00 in my bank account. You might call it an incredible act of faith. Some might call it being an idiot. That's okay. The reality, however, is that when we got married, we had to put an incredible amount of faith and dependency in God.

We weren't necessarily that young, either. I just turned 23 by 8-days. My wife, Grace, was 22-years-old. Although, we still had people attempting to speak into our lives saying our ages were "too young" to get married.

A life marked by Christ is a full life of dependency. It's dependency in every aspect of life, including the pursuit of marriage at an early age.

THREE: IT PROVES WE ARE MERE HUMAN IN OUR SEXUALITY.

Think about this logically with me for a minute. Young people start having sexual desires around eleven or twelve years of age. At this point, even if they wait until the preferred "getting out of college age" that is still 10-or-so years of living with strong sexual desires. That is one reason why marriage throughout history was much earlier.

In 1 Corinthians 7:8-9, Paul says, "But I say to the unmarried and to widows that it is good for them if they remain even as I. But if they do not have self-control, let them marry;

for it is better to marry than to burn with passion..."

According to Paul, a lack of self-control is actually one reason to get married, and I would argue that it is also one reason, in our culture, to get married at an early age.

FOUR: IT PROVES OUR DESIRE TO STAND AGAINST THE TIDE.

I don't have to convince you that the biblical foundation of marriage is under attack in our culture. Part of what it means to flourish as men and women is to embrace the roles that God has created for us.

Men and women are absolutely equal in dignity, value, and worth, but we are different in role and function. This means that we operate differently—biologically, physically, emotionally, and functionally.

When you as a young person embrace the pursuit of early marriage, you are standing firm on the Word of God by embracing the roles God has designed for you at an early age. By doing this, you are reflecting back to the world not only God's design for gender roles, but also God's design for marriage.

Your lifestyle then becomes the finest, Christ-centered apologetic to your closest family, friends, and neighbors (Jude 1).

FIVE: IT PROVES THAT GOD'S DESIGN FOR MARRIAGE IS NOT A CULTURAL BENCHMARK FOR YOUR LIFE.

So many of us have the pursuit of marriage backwards. We tend to think of the pursuit of marriage after these other cultural things happen in our life: go off to college, graduate college, get internships, get a master's degree, get a nice paying job, buy a house, have a 401(k), etc.

Only after all of these things are complete are we able to pursue marriage. This view puts marriage as just another thing to check off on your list of cultural benchmarks to accomplish in your life. Marriage, however, is quite the opposite.

Marriage is the oldest institution in history. It was in the Garden of Eden that God instituted marriage between one woman and one man (**Gen. 2:24**). It was a foreshadow of the greatest institution to come centuries later.

What is more, Paul doesn't call marriage a game, a sinking ship, an anchor in someone's life, or a thorn. No! He calls it a reflection of a great mystery (**Eph. 5:32**)—the mystery between Christ and his Bride.

And, my friends, it's still a good thing for you.

97